Writing Teacher's Handbook
Persuasive Writing

Written by June Hetzel and Deborah McIntire

"Everything goes back to this general
aim: to make students more effective
as human beings."
—Karin DeLong

(from *Slithery Snakes and Other Aides to Children's Writings*
by Walter T. Petty and Mary E. Bowen. Allyn & Bacon, Inc., 1972)

Illustrator: Corbin Hillam
Editor: Joel Kupperstein
Project Director: Carolea Williams

CTP ©1998, Creative Teaching Press, Inc., Cypress, CA 90630

Table of Contents

Introduction

Persuasive Writing is one resource in the *Writing Teacher's Handbook* four-book series that assists teachers of grades 4–6 in effectively implementing classroom writing programs. The lessons in each book include actual writing samples from upper-grade students.

Writing Domains

Each resource book in the *Writing Teacher's Handbook* series describes detailed lessons in one of the four writing domains—narrative, expressive, informative, and persuasive.

The *persuasive domain* involves convincing readers of beliefs and reasoning (e.g., persuasive essays, campaign speeches). The *narrative domain* focuses on telling a story (e.g., autobiographical incidents, short stories). The *expressive domain* includes poems and stories that express sensory detail and emotions (e.g., journal entries, haiku). The *informative domain* encompasses writing products that explain factual information (e.g., news articles, how-tos).

Many writing products fall within more than one domain. For example, a ballad describes a person's emotions (expressive) but also tells a story (narrative). A dialogue can evoke emotion (expressive), but can also depict one person trying to convince another of his or her opinion (persuasive). Emphasize the critical components of each writing product to help your students sharpen their writing skills and prepare them for writing success.

Lesson Plan Format

Lessons in this book include:

Critical Components—a list of the essential components of each writing product

Preparation—a description of what teachers need to do prior to the lesson

Setting the Stage—hints for introducing the lesson and engaging student interest

Instructional Input—directions for initiating a formal writing lesson and modeling the critical components of writing samples

Guided Practice—exercises for reinforcing the writing lesson

Independent Practice—activities to help students write independently

Presentation—ideas for organizing, publishing, and presenting student work

Teaching Hints/Extensions—tips to explore and extend the topic and writing domain

In addition, at the end of each section is a reproducible rubric for evaluating student work. Consider giving students the rubric at the beginning of the lesson so they can write with specific goals in mind.

The Writing Process

The writing process involves five steps: prewriting, writing a rough draft, revising, editing, and publishing/presenting the final product. These five steps are integral to any type of writing and form the foundation for all writing lessons in this book. Guide students through the stages of the process for each writing lesson, particularly the activities in the Independent Practice sections. Emphasize to students that they may need to repeat the cycle of revising and editing several times until their manuscript is ready for publication. Provide students with copies of the Writing Process Cards (page 13), and have them complete a card for each writing task and attach it to the final product. The first space for check-off in the Editing box of the Writing Process Card is for self-editing and the second is for peer or teacher editing.

Prewriting

Prewriting occurs after a thorough discussion of a topic but before formal writing about the topic. The prewriting stage is a structured brainstorming session aimed at eliciting spontaneous thinking about a specific topic. During the prewriting stage, help students use clusters and graphic organizers to organize their thoughts. For example, prewriting for a letter trying to convince someone to buy a puppy might include a simple cluster such as the following:

The central idea, the desire for a new puppy, becomes the basis for the topic sentence. The content of the cluster's spokes becomes the basis for supporting sentences.

All of the lessons in this book involve some sort of persuasion. Because changing how a person thinks about a particular issue can be difficult, the art of persuasive writing requires a great deal of skill. For example, the writer may attempt to persuade the reader (or listener) to buy a product, read a book, change his or her behavior, lower prices, or vote for a political candidate.

It is important for the writer to keep this in mind when planning the structure and approach of his or her writing product. Throughout this book, you will find graphic organizers that help students organize their thinking and address the critical components of each of their writing products.

After students complete the brainstorming session, have them skim over their prewriting work and trim unnecessary or irrelevant content. The remaining information forms the skeleton or framework of the project.

Rough Draft

The rough draft is the first round of organized writing. During rough-draft writing, students write spontaneously, following the organizational framework of the prewriting graphic organizer. Students should feel free to deviate from the skeletal framework of the prewriting organizer, as long as the requirements of the writing type (as defined by the rubric) are met. Frequently, the most creative writing comes from the spontaneity of a rough draft.

Students should not worry about precise spelling and punctuation while writing rough drafts. During the editing stage, however, spelling and punctuation should be fine-tuned to perfection!

Revising

The revising stage requires students to reorganize at four levels: the entire piece, each paragraph, each sentence, and each individual word. Encourage students to revise in this order to save time and, potentially, unnecessary work. For example, if a writer deletes an entire paragraph,

no time is wasted revising the sentences or words in that paragraph.

Revising the Entire Piece

At this level of revising, students look at the "big picture." They read and reread their writing, asking the following questions:

Does the piece flow from one idea to another?

Are paragraphs in a logical sequence?

Are there transitions between paragraphs?

Is the writing clear and understandable?

Are facts accurate and arguments sound?

Are there unnecessary facts and arguments that can be omitted?

Does the writing product meet the requirements of the rubric?

Revising Each Paragraph

In addition to larger organizational revising, students must revise their writing at the paragraph level. At this stage, students carefully examine each paragraph, asking the following:

Are sentences arranged in a logical order?

Is there a topic sentence?

Are there supporting sentences?

Have I avoided redundancy?

Does each paragraph add to the clarity, depth, and/or intensity of the piece?

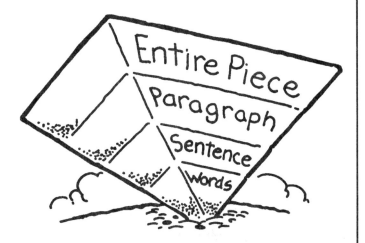

Revising Each Sentence

Students may wish to reorder or revise words within sentences to strengthen preciseness, add interest, and increase the effectiveness of their persuasive arguments.

> Weak Example:
> **I felt bad about the situation.**

> Strong Example:
> **My eyes swelled with tears over the situation.**

Word efficiency is another aspect of sentence revision. Students should be taught to use as few as words as necessary to relay the desired meaning.

> Weak Example:
> **The wood cabinet made of mahogany was beautiful, and we decided to buy it.**

> Strong Example:
> **We decided to buy the beautiful mahogany cabinet.**

Students may wish to incorporate the following persuasive techniques. These techniques are covered in detail on page 39.

Loaded Words: words and phrases that have a strong emotional impact

> ***Cleanall*** **kills deadly germs, protecting the lives of your loved ones.**

Endorsement: association with a respected organization or well-known person

> ***Skatefree*** **is the only skateboard used by world champion skater Emil Gold.**

Glittering Generality: association with something recognized as desirable

> **For a dazzling, healthy smile, use *Whiteall* Toothpaste.**

Bandwagon: appealing to the audience's desire not to be left out and stressing the "power in numbers" concept

> **Across the nation, people everywhere are discovering the power of *Magic Ax.***

Name Calling: statements or implications about wrong or inferior competition

> ***Fresh Breeze*** **styles hair more effectively than those cheap, sticky grocery store brands.**

Plain Folks: association with common people and common needs rather than with rich celebrities or privileged politicians

> **As a kindergarten teacher and mother of three, Christy works hard all day, every day. Only *Relief-Now* takes away her nagging backaches.**

Revising Individual Words

Revising at the word level constitutes fine-tuning. This is the time to have students pull out the thesaurus and dictionary. This is the time to polish!

Here are some tips for revising at the word level:

Use interesting words—

> **Weak Example:**
> **The decorated shirt was pretty.**

> **Strong Example:**
> **The rhinestone-studded shirt dazzled everyone.**

Strengthen verbs—

> **Weak Example:**
> **She ate her dinner.**

> **Strong Example:**
> **She devoured her dinner.**

Clarify pronouns—

> **Weak Example:**
> **He met him at the park.**

> **Strong Example:**
> **Mr. Hetzel met Nathaniel at Lemon Grove Park.**

Clarify vague concepts—

> **Weak Example:**
> **Mr. Myers and Jennifer played a game.**

> **Strong Example:**
> **Mr. Myers and Jennifer played soccer.**

Use sensory detail to evoke emotion—

> **Weak Example:**
> **She was sad.**

> **Strong Example:**
> **She couldn't hide her tear-stained cheeks and muffled sobs.**

Editing

At the editing stage, students make sure words are spelled correctly and punctuation is accurate. Here are some hints for this ongoing area of growth.

Editing Marks

Photocopy the Editing Marks reproducible (page 14) for students to refer to as they complete this stage of the writing process. Be sure students are familiar with and comfortable using editing symbols before beginning their first writing-process piece.

Spelling

Be sure students keep ongoing personal dictionaries in which they record new words they encounter. Included in these dictionaries should be a list of the most commonly used words in their writing. Also, be sure students have access to comprehensive dictionaries and thesauruses. Reinforce the idea that students may need to repeat the editing stage for any particular writing project.

If your students write using a computer, teach them how to use programs that check spelling. However, be sure that they clearly understand that computers will not detect missing words or homophone errors.

Punctuation

Mastering punctuation can be challenging. Teach punctuation as you teach writing, starting with the basics (ending punctuation and capitalization) and moving to commas, semicolons, and colons as students gain mastery. Do not expect perfection at the rough-draft stage. The goal of teaching writing is to help students improve their writing with each revision.

Repeated Reading

Students often have the misconception that one round of reading is sufficient in editing a piece. Encourage several reads by several people (the author, peers, and adults). Each reading provides an opportunity to improve the writing. For peer editing, students might engage in a round robin discussion or an "author's chair," where one student reads a piece to the group or class and solicits constructive feedback.

Publishing/Presenting

The most rewarding aspect of the writing process is the final draft, or publishing/presenting stage. At this point, the writer finally sees his or her completed work in polished form, available for others' enjoyment. Provide forums for students to read their writing to one another, to other classes, and to parents. Encourage students to bind their writing into books and submit copies to school and classroom libraries. Students may also want to submit their work to local newspapers for publication. Tape-record stories for reading centers and post students' writing in your classroom on bulletin board displays.

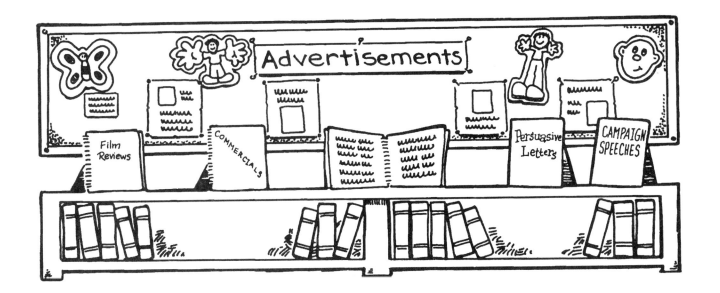

Writing Devices

Certain literary devices can increase the effectiveness and quality of students' writing. These devices include alliteration, metaphor, simile, sensory detail, onomatopoeia, and personification. Review these devices throughout your writing lessons, particularly during the revising stage. Challenge students to locate these devices in their independent reading materials.

Alliteration

Increase students' understanding of how alliteration—a string of words with the same initial sound—enhances the "sound" of language. Read and recite classic tongue twisters *(Peter Piper picked a peck of pickled peppers),* make up original tongue twisters *(Rhonda Rhino wrestled raggedy Rita Rhino),* and brainstorm phrases that include repetitive initial sounds *(Sally's savory sweets, Dominating Dominic,* and *Veronica Victor's venom).* Challenge students to complete these alliterative phrases and use alliteration in their writing. The use of alliteration is especially effective in advertisements, where alliterative slogans and product names make the product more memorable to the audience.

Metaphor

Increase students' ability to relay meaning to a reader by comparing two ideas using "word pictures," or metaphors. Read some ordinary sentences and enhance the meaning of the sentences by rewriting them using metaphors.

Weak Example:
The manuscript has a lot of good qualities and can be improved.

Strong Example:
The manuscript is a diamond in the rough.

Weak Example:
The young man is very strong and one day will be in the Olympics.

Strong Example:
Such a young Hercules will one day compete in the Olympics.

Simile

Similar to metaphor, a simile compares two ideas using *as* or *like*. Help students enjoy similes by reading *Quick As a Cricket* by Audrey Wood. Discuss simile examples in the book, such as "quick as a cricket" and "strong as an ox." Discuss how similes evoke images that enhance the mental pictures of what the writer is trying to relate.

Sensory Detail

Writers who use sensory detail (words and phrases that vividly describe sight, sound, smell, taste, and touch) involve the reader's senses and add interest to their writing.

Weak Example:
I felt hot and tired after the race through the desert.

Strong Example:
Every inch of my body ached after the grueling race through the scorching, arid desert.

Onomatopoeia

Onomatopoeic words represent the sounds of the things they describe, for example, *crunch, crackle,* and *bang.* These words help clarify readers' mental images and intensify events and emotions.

Weak Example:
I heard a loud sound come from next door.

Strong Example:
Bang! The explosive sound pierced the air.

Weak Example:
The magician made the object disappear.

Strong Example:
Poof! With a swish of the magician's wand, the object disappeared.

Personification

Personification is the assigning of human characteristics to a nonhuman object. To provide students practice with this device, guide them in brainstorming a list of objects and the human characteristics that could describe them. Then, create sentences using items from this personification list. For example, students might use the word *shy* to describe the moon. Then, they might write the sentence *The moon shyly peeked through the clouds.*

Assessment

Each lesson in this resource includes a rubric for evaluating student work. These rubrics allow readers to assess the critical components, style issues, originality, and mechanics of the work. Some also include space for readers' comments.

Rubrics are valuable tools at all stages of the writing process. Give the rubrics to students as they begin prewriting to help them understand the criteria by which their work will be assessed. At this early stage, rubrics also help students understand the focus and purpose of each writing genre.

As students revise their own work, rubrics help them assess the quality of what they have written. Have students complete a rubric for each draft they write and include detailed comments each time. Also, have peer editors complete rubrics when evaluating classmates' work. Objectively evaluating one's own work is a difficult task, to be sure. Give students practice evaluating each other's work. When students make tactful, constructive comments, they contribute to the improvement of each other's writing.

Rubrics also give you a standardized format for the final assessment of students' writing. Ask students to attach all of their completed rubrics to each project they turn in. Use the student-completed rubrics to assess the progress students made while writing.

When you complete the final rubric and present it to students, they will clearly understand why they received the grades they were given.

As students complete writing projects, you may want to store their work in portfolios. Whether your portfolios are simple file folders in a file cabinet or decorated pizza boxes in which students can store artwork that accompanies their writing, be sure students have open access to them. Invite students to add at any time work they feel shows growth or excellence. Review these portfolios when determining students' writing grades, and have them available for parents to look through at Open House and at parent-teacher conferences.

Writing Process Cards

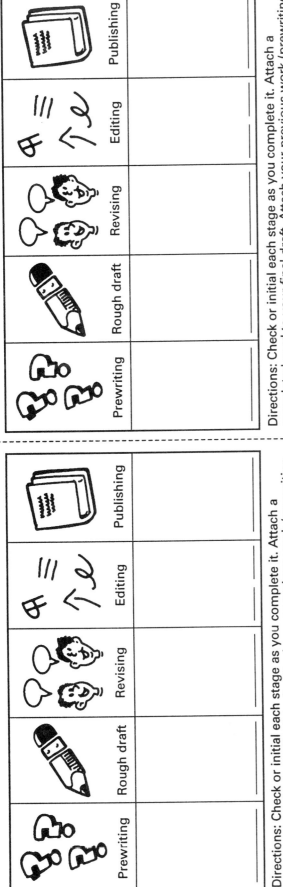

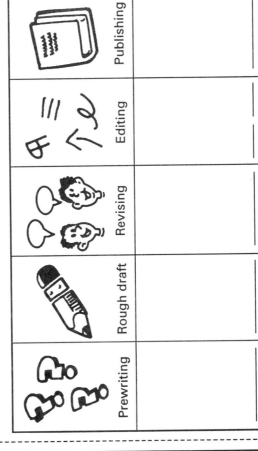

Prewriting	Rough draft	Revising	Editing	Publishing

Directions: Check or initial each stage as you complete it. Attach a completed card to your final draft. Attach your previous work (prewriting, rough draft, revising, and editing pages) behind your final draft to show the stages of your writing process.

Prewriting	Rough draft	Revising	Editing	Publishing

Directions: Check or initial each stage as you complete it. Attach a completed card to your final draft. Attach your previous work (prewriting, rough draft, revising, and editing pages) behind your final draft to show the stages of your writing process.

Prewriting	Rough draft	Revising	Editing	Publishing

Directions: Check or initial each stage as you complete it. Attach a completed card to your final draft. Attach your previous work (prewriting, rough draft, revising, and editing pages) behind your final draft to show the stages of your writing process.

Prewriting	Rough draft	Revising	Editing	Publishing

Directions: Check or initial each stage as you complete it. Attach a completed card to your final draft. Attach your previous work (prewriting, rough draft, revising, and editing pages) behind your final draft to show the stages of your writing process.

Editing Marks

Editing Mark	Examples in Text	Meaning
≡	watch out!	Capitalize the letter.
/	Come here Øuickly.	Use lowercase.
∧	Look at that girafe. (f)	Insert a letter. (This symbol is called a caret.)
⊙	Place a period here ⊙	Insert a period.
⌃	When it rains the geraniums love it.	Insert a comma.
¶	. . . with me. The next day . . .	Start a new paragraph.
⌄ ⌄	"Good morning, Sally called.	Insert quotations.
‿	pop corn	Join words.
ℓ	June and and Deborah wrote this book.	Delete this word.
∧	Luella Carolea like it. (and)	Insert a word.
∽	Can you with come me?	Reverse word order.
#	Make a wise decision.	Insert a space.

14

Fiction Book Review

Critical Components

A fiction book review begins with "the basics": the title, the author, and the type of book. A fiction book review provides information about setting, character development, and plot, but does not give away the ending. A fiction book review discusses the author's writing style and compares the book with similar books written by the same author or other authors. A fiction book review includes the reviewer's opinions and recommendations, sometimes in the form of a rating scale.

Preparation

Look for reviews of children's books in your local newspaper, bookstore, library, or in children's magazines and bring several of them to class. Try to find at least one review that covers a book the majority of your class has read. If this is not possible, write a review of a book your class has read together. (Use the Fiction Book Review Frame on page 20 to assist you.) Encourage students to locate and bring book reviews to class as well. Make overhead transparencies of pages 18 and 19. Photocopy pages 20 and 21 for students.

Setting the Stage

Read aloud the book review you located or wrote. Discuss the reviewer's opinion, rating, and recommendation. Take a class vote to see how many students agree with the reviewer's opinions. Allow time for students to discuss and debate how they feel about the review.

Instructional Input

1. Use the overhead transparency of page 18 to introduce the critical components of a fiction book review.

2. As you discuss each component, write it at the top of a piece of tagboard or construction paper. Post these across the front of the room.

Guided Practice

1. Display the overhead transparency of the Fiction Book Review Sample (page 19). Read the review aloud and ask students to identify the critical components. Label each component using an overhead pen.

2. Divide the class into small groups. Give each group one or more of the book reviews you collected. Invite groups to read the reviews and cut out statements that fit into the critical components categories. Have students tape the statements onto the appropriate charts. Allow time for discussion and comparison of review components.

• The Pearls of Lutra by Brian Jacques •
Student Reviewer: Miki E. Fujieda

title, author, genre, setting

The Pearls of Lutra, by Brian Jacques, is the ninth thrilling fantasy of the Redwall series. This story takes place between Redwall Abbey, Mossflower Woods, and the Island of Sampetra, far across the sea.

plot characters

The pearls were stolen from the tribe of Lutra by sea rats, but now the six pearls are all hidden in Redwall Abbey. Tansy, a curious hedge-maid, decides to take a peek in an old attic and finds a pearl and a riddle to look for the rest of them. Because Tansy is loved and trusted by all, her friends are eager to join her in her search. Helping her is a wise old vole named Rollo and a lively squirrel maid named Cracklyn. The three friends are determined to find the Pearls of Lutra.

Meanwhile, the Abbot of Redwall gets kidnapped, and Martin and his little band of warriors have to save him.

no giveaway

Is the Abbot never going to see his abbey again, or can Martin and his band of warriors save him? Is Tansy going to find all the pearls, or are the sea rats going to find them first? Find out in The Pearls of Lutra.

opinions and recommendations

I really liked this book because it has lots of adventure and because it's not like a fairy tale where everything and everyone always turns out all right. Because some of the characters get injured or die, I don't recommend this book for small children. Everyone else should rush out and get this book from the library or bookstore! You won't be sorry.

Independent Practice

1. Invite students to write their own review of a recently read fiction book. Have them use the Fiction Book Review Frame (page 20) to organize their thoughts prior to writing.

2. Invite students to use the Fiction Book Review Rubric (page 21) to self-evaluate their work.

Presentation

- Display student reviews on a bulletin board or bind them in a book titled *Room ___'s Rave Reviews*.

- Consider starting a class book-review box or website. Give students the ongoing opportunity to write reviews on index cards and keep them in a box or record them on a website. Make these reviews readily accessible to other students so they can assess their peers' opinions before they read a book.

- Create a videotape library of fiction book reviews by videotaping each review as students present them orally. Create a separate videotape for each genre.

- Encourage students to create an appropriate book jacket design for the book they reviewed. Display these book jackets next to matching student reviews on a bulletin board display.

Teaching Hints and Extensions

- Invite students to survey their classmates to determine the class's favorite books. Compile a top-ten list and post the list on a bulletin board.

- Brainstorm with students interesting words that can be used to express approval or disapproval when writing reviews. Display this list on a "word wall" and have students add to it as they discover new words.

Fiction Book Review Components

CONTENT INFORMATION

A fiction book review provides information about

- the setting (when and where the story takes place)
- character development (how the author lets the reader know about a character's personality)
- plot (the main action of the story, including the major conflict)

Note: A review should not give away how the problem is solved.

AUTHOR'S STYLE

A fiction book review discusses anything unique or interesting about the author's writing style, such as use of humor, descriptive phrases, clever dialogue, and fast-paced action. A comparison to a similar book by the same author or another author strengthens the review.

OPINIONS AND RECOMMENDATIONS

A fiction book review recommends the book to a specific audience (the type of person who would enjoy this book) and includes an overall rating (why you liked or disliked the book and a rating such as "thumbs up" or "three stars").

Persuasive Writing © 1998 Creative Teaching Press

Fiction Book Review Sample

• *The Pearls of Lutra* by Brian Jacques •

Student Reviewer: Miki E. Fujieda

The Pearls of Lutra, by Brian Jacques, is the ninth thrilling fantasy of the Redwall series. This story takes place between Redwall Abbey, Mossflower Woods, and the Island of Sampetra, far across the sea.

The pearls were stolen from the tribe of Lutra by sea rats, but now the six pearls are all hidden in Redwall Abbey. Tansy, a curious hedgehog maid, decides to take a peek in an old attic and finds a pearl and a riddle to look for the rest of them. Because Tansy is loved and trusted by all, her friends are eager to join her in her search. Helping her is a wise old vole named Rollo and a lively squirrel maid named Cracklyn. The three friends are determined to find the Pearls of Lutra.

Meanwhile, the Abbot of Redwall gets kidnapped, and Martin and his little band of warriors have to save him.

Is the Abbot never going to see his abbey again, or can Martin and his band of warriors save him? Is Tansy going to find all the pearls, or are the sea rats going to find them first? Find out in *The Pearls of Lutra*.

I really liked this book because it has lots of adventure and because it's not like a fairy tale where everything and everyone always turns out all right. Because some of the characters get injured or die, I don't recommend this book for small children. Everyone else should rush out and get this book from the library or bookstore! You won't be sorry.

Name: _____

Fiction Book Review Frame

THE BASICS

Title: _____

Author: _____

Genre: What type of book is it?_____

CONTENT INFORMATION

Setting: Where does the story take place? _____

Character Development: How does the author help us know the characters?_____

_____

Plot: What happens in the story? What is the major conflict? _____

_____

Author's Style: What is unusual or interesting about the author's writing? _____

_____

OPINIONS AND RECOMMENDATIONS

Intended Audience: What type of person would like this book? _____

_____

Overall Rating: Why did you like or dislike this book? Would you recommend it?
How do you rate it?

_____

_____

_____

Persuasive Writing © 1998 Creative Teaching Press

Fiction Book Review Rubric

	Great!	O.K.	Needs Help
Critical Components			
Includes "the basics": book title, author, and genre			
Provides information about the setting, character development, and plot (doesn't give away ending)			
Discusses author's writing style			
Compares the book to other similar books			
Gives opinions and recommendations			
Style			
Word Choice Strong, active verbs			
Precise words			
Words that evoke imagery and sensory detail			
Writing devices such as alliteration, metaphor, simile, onomatopoeia, and personification			
Coherence Clearly presented ideas			
Logically sequenced ideas			
Mechanics			
Ending punctuation			
Capitalization			
Comma rules			
Quotation marks			
Paragraph structure			

Comments

_____

_____

_____

Persuasive Writing © 1998 Creative Teaching Press

Film Review

Critical Components

A film review states the reviewer's opinion about the movie and provides information about the film's genre (type of film), story line (basic plot), director (person in charge of producing the film), acting and actors, cinematography (visual appearance and effects), musical score, special effects, and intended audience (who would enjoy this film). A film review includes an overall rating of the film.

Preparation

Obtain reviews of age- and content-appropriate movies in your local newspaper. Bring several to class on the day of the lesson. Encourage students to locate reviews that critique films they have seen or would like to see. Invite them to bring the reviews to class on the day of the lesson. (You may want to screen these first.) Make an overhead transparency of page 25. Photocopy pages 26 and 27 for students.

Setting the Stage

Divide students into small groups. Provide each group with a published film review. Instruct students to read and discuss the review, looking for similarities and differences between film reviews and book reviews.

Instructional Input

1. Draw a Venn diagram on the board and label the circles *Film Review* and *Book Review.* Elicit from students similarities and differences between the two types of reviews. As students mention components of a film review not present in a book review (director, cinematography, acting, and special effects), make sure they understand each term and its significance in producing a film.

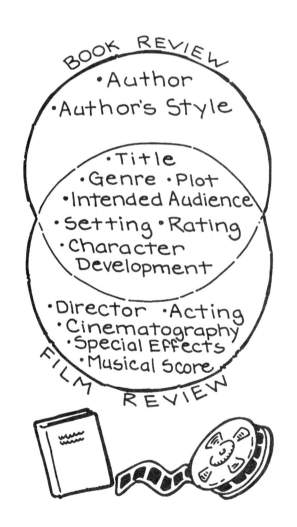

BOOK REVIEW
- Author
- Author's Style

- Title
- Genre • Plot
- Intended Audience
- Setting • Rating
- Character Development

- Director • Acting
- Cinematography
- Special Effects
- Musical Score

FILM REVIEW

Guided Practice

1. Display the overhead transparency of the Film Review Sample (page 25). As a class, identify and label the critical components of a film review.

2. Have students return to their small groups. Provide each group with a copy of the Film Review Frame (page 26). Invite students to record the information provided in their published review to complete the frame.

Independent Practice

1. Provide each student with another copy of the Film Review Frame. Show a film in class such as *The Secret Garden, Sarah Plain and Tall*, or a film related to a social studies unit.

2. During the film, have students take notes on the frame. After the film, allow time for discussion of their notes and opinions of the film.

3. Have students use their frames to write a complete review of the film.

4. Have students share their reviews in small groups. Encourage group members to complete the Film Review Rubric (page 27) to provide peer feedback for one another.

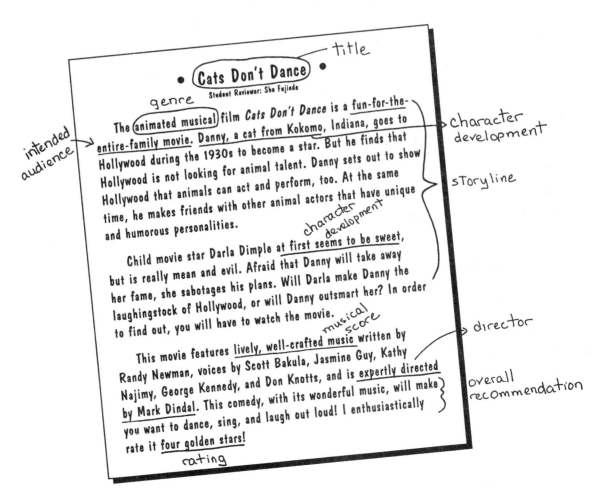

title

• Cats Don't Dance •

Student Reviewer: Sho Fujieda

genre

intended audience

The (animated musical) film *Cats Don't Dance* is a fun-for-the-entire-family movie. Danny, a cat from Kokomo, Indiana, goes to Hollywood during the 1930s to become a star. But he finds that Hollywood is not looking for animal talent. Danny sets out to show Hollywood that animals can act and perform, too. At the same time, he makes friends with other animal actors that have unique and humorous personalities.

character development

storyline

Child movie star Darla Dimple at first seems to be sweet, but is really mean and evil. Afraid that Danny will take away her fame, she sabotages his plans. Will Darla make Danny the laughingstock of Hollywood, or will Danny outsmart her? In order to find out, you will have to watch the movie.

character development

This movie features lively, well-crafted music written by Randy Newman, voices by Scott Bakula, Jasmine Guy, Kathy Najimy, George Kennedy, and Don Knotts, and is expertly directed by Mark Dindal. This comedy, with its wonderful music, will make you want to dance, sing, and laugh out loud! I enthusiastically rate it four golden stars!

musical score

director

overall recommendation

rating

Presentation

- Invite each student to design a poster to advertise the film he or she reviewed. Encourage students to include in their reviews persuasive language and propaganda techniques. Display the posters and reviews on a bulletin board.

- Create a bulletin board that includes a film reel canister mounted on the wall and a strip of film coming out of the canister. Create a strip of enlarged frames to highlight reviews posted on the bulletin board.

Teaching Hints/Extensions

- Whenever students see new films, invite them to write brief film reviews on index cards. Alphabetize and store these reviews in a file box labeled *Room ____'s Film Reviews.* Make the reviews accessible to the class as a reference for movie recommendations.

- Students can work with partners to develop interview questions for the director of the film they reviewed. Have them also suggest answers the director might give and share this information with the class in the form of a play-acted talk show interview.

Film Review Sample

• Cats Don't Dance •

Student Reviewer: Sho Fujieda

The animated musical film *Cats Don't Dance* is a fun-for-the-entire-family movie. Danny, a cat from Kokomo, Indiana, goes to Hollywood during the 1930s to become a star. But he finds that Hollywood is not looking for animal talent. Danny sets out to show Hollywood that animals can act and perform, too. At the same time, he makes friends with other animal actors that have unique and humorous personalities.

Child movie star Darla Dimple at first seems to be sweet, but is really mean and evil. Afraid that Danny will take away her fame, she sabotages his plans. Will Darla make Danny the laughingstock of Hollywood, or will Danny outsmart her? In order to find out, you will have to watch the movie.

This movie features lively, well-crafted music written by Randy Newman, voices by Scott Bakula, Jasmine Guy, Kathy Najimy, George Kennedy, and Don Knotts, and is expertly directed by Mark Dindal. This comedy, with its wonderful music, will make you want to dance, sing, and laugh out loud! I enthusiastically rate it four golden stars!

Name: _____

Film Review Frame

Genre: What type of movie is this? (e.g., western, comedy, drama)	**Story Line:** What is the basic plot? Is the plot believable? Did it hold your interest? Do the events flow in a logical sequence?
Director: Who is the director? Does he or she keep the pace of the film interesting? What techniques does he or she use to make the film unique?	**Acting:** Who are the actors in this film? Are they well-cast? Is the acting natural and believable?
Cinematography: Is the photography natural and believable? Do you feel like you're actually there?	**Musical Score and Special Effects:** Are the special effects appropriate and believable? Does the background music add to the movie?
Intended Audience: Who would like this movie? Is it appropriate for all ages?	**Overall Rating:** Do you recommend this movie? Why or why not?

Persuasive Writing © 1998 Creative Teaching Press

Writer's Name: _____   Evaluator's Name: _____

Film Review Rubric

	Great!	O.K.	Needs Help
Critical Components			
Includes "the basics": film title, screenwriter, and genre			
Provides information about the setting, plot (story line), character development, and acting quality			
Discusses director's techniques			
Discusses musical score and cinematography (including special effects)			
Compares the movie to other similar movies			
Gives an overall rating			
Style			
Word Choice Strong, active verbs			
Precise words			
Words that evoke imagery and sensory detail			
Writing devices such as alliteration, metaphor, simile, onomatopoeia, and personification			
Coherence Clearly presented ideas			
Logically sequenced ideas			
Mechanics			
Ending punctuation			
Capitalization			
Comma rules			
Quotation marks			
Paragraph			

Comments

_____

_____

Advertisement

Critical Components

An advertisement's product has a clever, memorable name. An advertisement describes the special features of the product. An advertisement uses persuasive words and phrases. An advertisement establishes a sense of urgency. An advertisement makes it clear that the product is affordable.

Preparation

Collect copies of three or four ads so that each student can read and critique the same samples. Ask students to look through magazines and catalogs and cut out advertisements they feel convince them to buy a product or service. Request that students bring the ads to class on the day of the lesson. Make sure students' ads are appropriate. Make overhead transparencies of pages 31 and 32. Photocopy pages 33–35 for students.

Setting the Stage

Have students share the advertisements they cut out of magazines and catalogs. Ask students about the products or services their ads describe. Record product names on the board. Then, have a few students read their ads aloud. Ask the class the following questions:

What special product or service features were described in the ad?

What words made the product or service sound appealing?

Did the ad establish a strong need or desire for the product or service?

Was a sense of urgency established?

If a price for the product or service was listed, was it reasonable?

Instructional Input

1. Help students discover the critical features of a good advertisement by writing the critical components on the board and listing examples for each one.

Critical Components

Product Names	Special Features	Persuasive Words and Phrases	Sense of Urgency Established	Affordable Prices

Guided Practice

1. Give students copies of advertisements you have collected. Help them identify the critical features of the advertisements by having them circle and label the features on their papers.

2. Show students the overhead transparencies of pages 31 and 32. Have them verbally identify the critical components in the manner shown below.

3. Give students copies of the Advertisement Sample 3 reproducible (page 33). Ask them to again read, circle, and label the critical features for both advertisements. Guide them through each ad. Have them identify any missing critical components.

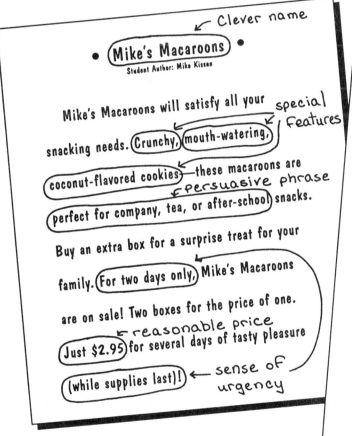

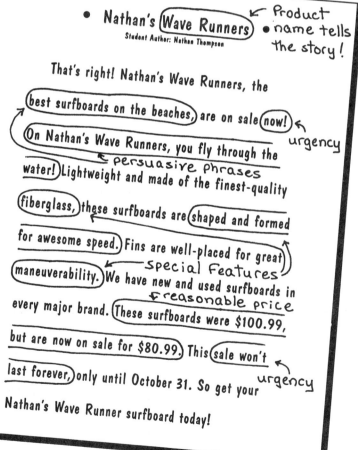

Independent Practice

1. Ask students to use the Advertisement Frame (page 34) to brainstorm the content of their first draft.

2. Before students write their first draft, provide them with copies of the Advertisement Rubric (page 35). This way, expectations are clear for the student. As the student moves through the writing process, he or she can return to the rubric to see that all critical components are in place and revise and edit as necessary. Using the rubric, the student self-assesses several times before experiencing peer, parent, or teacher critiques.

3. Encourage students to include an illustration with their final ad text.

Presentation

- Invite students to design ad collages, combining written and illustrated advertisements that relate to similar product types, such as cars, soap, and clothing.

- Combine student ads into a classroom magazine. Encourage students to illustrate their products and services. Consider making additional copies to submit to the school library or other classroom libraries.

Teaching Hints/Extensions

- Invite each student to create a clever product name that includes alliteration, onomatopoeia, or rhyme. Then, have students work with partners to write ads for each other's product.

- Encourage students to become attuned to their "audience," their customers. Have students write several ads for the same product and survey their classmates as to which ad is the most convincing and why. Ask them to report their findings to the class.

- Invite students to design an ad campaign for an upcoming school fund-raiser. Challenge them to incorporate appropriate advertising techniques (see page 39) into their campaign.

Advertisement
Sample 1

• Mike's Macaroons •
Student Author: Mike Kissen

Mike's Macaroons will satisfy all your snacking needs. Crunchy, mouth-watering, coconut-flavored cookies—these macaroons are perfect for company, tea, or after-school snacks. Buy an extra box for a surprise treat for your family. For two days only, Mike's Macaroons are on sale! Two boxes for the price of one. Just $2.95 for several days of tasty pleasure (while supplies last)!

Advertisement
Sample 2

• Nathan's Wave Runners •
Student Author: Nathan Thompson

That's right! Nathan's Wave Runners, the best surfboards on the beaches, are on sale now! On Nathan's Wave Runners, you fly through the water! Lightweight and made of the finest-quality fiberglass, these surfboards are shaped and formed for awesome speed. Fins are well-placed for great maneuverability. We have new and used surfboards in every major brand. These surfboards were $100.99, but are now on sale for $80.99. This sale won't last forever, only until October 31. So get your Nathan's Wave Runner surfboard today!

Name: _____

Advertisement
Sample 3

• Slice-O-Matic •
Student Author: Jeffery Van Hoose

Do you ever get tired of chopping and peeling vegetables? Do you wish there was an easier way to do these things? Ladies and Gentlemen, the Slice-O-Matic! It slices; it peels. All you have to do is put the vegetables into the machine and push *slice* or *peel*. The Slice-O-Matic is guaranteed to make your job easier and has a two-year warranty. The Slice-O-Matic originally sold for $19.95, but now is $10.95, plus shipping and handling and any tax that might apply. Order your Slice-O-Matic while supplies last!

• Bubble Blast •
Student Author: Katrina Rallis

Bubble Blast will meet all your body-cleaning needs, including shampoo and body wash. You have a choice between peach or strawberry fragrance. We have interviewed three people who have tried Bubble Blast. The first customer said she loved the sweet smell and the soothing feeling. The second customer spread the news to all of her friends and relatives telling them how inexpensive it was for such a quality product. Our last customer told us she received many compliments on how lovely her hair looked and how fresh and clean she smelled. So, as you can see, Bubble Blast is a fantastic product and enjoyable to have in your bathroom. And now, for a limited time, if you buy two cans for the regular price, you get the third free! We are so sure you will love Bubble Blast that if you are not satisfied, you can return the product for a full refund. So buy your Bubble Blast today!

Advertisement Frame

1. Write a clever, memorable name for the product you wish to advertise.

_____

2. Describe the special features of this product.

a. _____

b. _____

c. _____

3. Brainstorm persuasive words and phrases to influence people to purchase your product.

4. Write a sentence that establishes a sense of urgency for people to purchase your product.

_____

_____

_____

5. Decide on a price that will make the product affordable and yet takes into account production costs and earning your company a profit.

_____

Persuasive Writing © 1998 Creative Teaching Press

Writer's Name: _____   Evaluator's Name: _____

Advertisement Rubric

	Great!	O.K.	Needs Help
Critical Components			
Includes a clever, memorable product name			
Describes the special features of the product			
Uses persuasive words and phrases			
Establishes a sense of urgency			
Makes clear that the product is affordable			
Style			
Word Choice Strong, active verbs			
Precise words			
Words that evoke imagery and sensory detail			
Writing devices such as alliteration, metaphor, simile, onomatopoeia, and personification			
Coherence Clearly presented ideas			
Logically sequenced ideas			
Other Considerations			
Originality			
Characterization			
Dialogue			
Mechanics			
Ending punctuation			
Capitalization			
Comma rules			
Quotation marks			
Paragraph structure			

Radio/Television Commercial

Critical Components

A commercial provides positive information about a person, product, or service aimed at persuading the audience to buy the product or endorse the person. A commercial uses persuasive language and advertising techniques (catchy name, special features, sense of urgency, affordable prices). A commercial often uses one or more propaganda techniques ("loaded" words, endorsement, glittering generalities, bandwagon, name-calling, plain-folks). A commercial is written for a short, condensed time period (15–60 seconds). A commercial provides staging information (setting/overview, actors or spokespeople, music, and mood) listed before the text of the commercial itself.

Preparation

Tape several commercials from radio or television that include a variety of the propaganda techniques discussed in the lesson. Ask local radio and television stations for old scripts and storyboards for real commercials. If possible, collect several commercials for similar products. Invite students to record commercials that effectively convince them to purchase a product or service. Encourage students to bring the tapes to class on the day of the lesson. Make overhead transparencies of pages 39–41. Photocopy pages 42 and 43 for students.

Setting the Stage

As you play the tapes of the commercials you and your students collected, challenge students to listen for attributes that make the commercials effective or ineffective. After watching the commercials, discuss these attributes with your students and invite them to vote on which products they would purchase and to support their votes with reasons.

Instructional Input

1. Review the student-authored advertisements from the preceding lesson. Identify any advertisement techniques used in these ads as well as in the commercials brought to class. Chart these techniques on the board.

2. Use the Propaganda Techniques overhead transparency (page 39) to introduce and teach techniques advertisers use to promote products. After you have discussed each technique, review the commercials again, stopping after each one to identify the propaganda techniques used.

3. Tell students that before writing the dialogue for their commercial, they need to include staging information about the setting, background music and sounds, and the mood they are seeking to generate.

Guided Practice

1. Display the overhead transparencies of the student-authored sample commercial scripts on pages 40 and 41. Discuss what information the authors provided before beginning the text of their commercials.

2. Have students identify and label any advertising and/or propaganda techniques used.

Independent Practice

1. Divide the class into small groups. Provide each group with an assortment of miscellaneous gadgets and materials, such as string, rubber bands, cork boards, unusual kitchen items, and items from science kits. Invite students to work in their groups to name this product and write a commercial advertising it. Provide each group with the Commercial Frame (page 42) to help them organize their thoughts.

2. Invite students to share their inventions and their ideas for commercials with the class.

3. Have each student independently write a 30–60 second TV or radio commercial that advertises a product or service. This can be a made-up product or one that is currently on the market. Provide students with the Commercial Frame (page 42) to assist them.

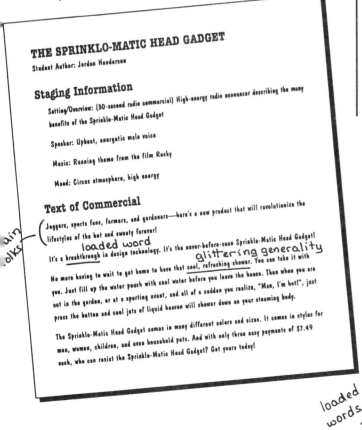

THE SPRINKLO-MATIC HEAD GADGET
Student Author: Jordan Henderson

Staging Information

Setting/Overview: (30-second radio commercial) High-energy radio announcer describing the many benefits of the Sprinklo-Matic Head Gadget

Speaker: Upbeat, energetic male voice

Music: Running theme from the film Rocky

Mood: Circus atmosphere, high energy

Text of Commercial

Joggers, sports fans, farmers, and gardeners—here's a new product that will revolutionize the lifestyles of the hot and sweaty forever! *loaded word* It's a breakthrough in design technology. It's the never-before-seen Sprinklo-Matic Head Gadget! *glittering generality*

No more having to wait to get home to have that cool, refreshing shower. You can take it with you. Just fill up the water pouch with cool water before you leave the house. Then when you are out in the garden, or at a sporting event, and all of a sudden you realize, "Man, I'm hot!", just press the button and cool jets of liquid heaven will shower down on your steaming body.

The Sprinklo-Matic Head Gadget comes in many different colors and sizes. It comes in styles for men, women, children, and even household pets. And with only three easy payments of $7.49 each, who can resist the Sprinklo-Matic Head Gadget? Get yours today!

plain folks

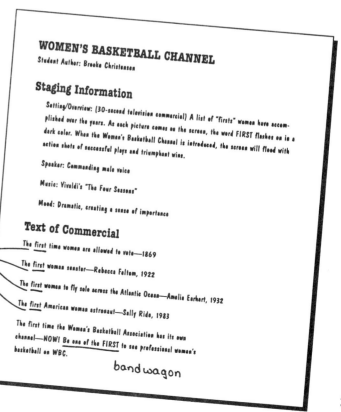

WOMEN'S BASKETBALL CHANNEL
Student Author: Brooke Christensen

Staging Information

Setting/Overview: (30-second television commercial) A list of "firsts" women have accomplished over the years. As each picture comes on the screen, the word FIRST flashes on in a dark color. When the Women's Basketball Channel is introduced, the screen will flood with action shots of successful plays and triumphant wins.

Speaker: Commanding male voice

Music: Vivaldi's "The Four Seasons"

Mood: Dramatic, creating a sense of importance

Text of Commercial

The first time women are allowed to vote—1869

The first woman senator—Rebecca Feltom, 1922

The first woman to fly solo across the Atlantic Ocean—Amelia Earhart, 1932

The first American woman astronaut—Sally Ride, 1983

The first time the Women's Basketball Association has its own channel—NOW! Be one of the FIRST to see professional women's basketball on WBC.

loaded words

bandwagon

Presentation

- Invite students to perform their commercials for the class or prepare an audiotape or videotape and share the finished product with the class. Have students write on three index cards (one phrase per card) *I want it!, I'm thinking about it,* and *Not a chance!* After they have viewed each commercial, have students hold up the card that reflects how convinced they were to buy the product or service.

- Videotape students' commercials to create a tape library that can be played at Open House and made available for check out.

Teaching Hints/Extensions

- Invite students to create a consumer guide about commonly purchased products. Have students test the products and then develop their own consumer reports to be compiled into a class consumer guide. Ask them to include in their reports information about price, availability, and usefulness, and comparisons with similar products.

- Encourage students to become wise decision-makers and to think critically before buying a product or supporting a cause. Ask them to list the products they purchased in the last month and record the advertising techniques and propaganda used to convince them to purchase these products.

- Examine with students the role of slogans and jingles in commercials. Because jingles are memorable and pleasing to the ear, they are often used in commercials. Invite students to go on a jingle hunt to collect and analyze contemporary slogans and jingles.

Propaganda Techniques

Propaganda is any attempt to persuade an audience to do something or believe something. Propaganda can be a powerful persuasive tool and is often used in advertisements and commercials. The following list includes some of the most commonly used techniques.

"Loaded" Words Words and phrases that have a strong emotional impact.

Without loaded words:
Cleanall **kills germs.**

With loaded words:
Cleanall **kills deadly germs, protecting the lives of your loved ones.**

Endorsement Associating the product or service with a well-known organization or person.

Skatefree **is the only skateboard used by world champion skater Emil Gold.**

Glittering Generality Associating the product with something recognized as desirable.

For a dazzling, healthy smile, use *Whiteall* **Toothpaste.**

Bandwagon Stressing the idea that people do not want to be left out.

Across the nation, people everywhere are discovering the power of *Magic Ax.*

Name Calling Stating or implying that the competition is wrong or inferior.

Fresh Breeze **styles hair better than those cheap, sticky grocery store brands.**

Plain Folks Identifying the product with common people and common needs rather than with rich celebrities or privileged politicians.

As a kindergarten teacher and mother of three, Christy works hard all day, every day. Only *Relief Now* **takes away her nagging backaches.**

Persuasive Writing © 1998 Creative Teaching Press

Commercial
Sample 1

WOMEN'S BASKETBALL CHANNEL

Student Author: Brooke Christensen

Staging Information

Setting/Overview: (30-second television commercial) A list of "firsts" women have accomplished over the years. As each picture comes on the screen, the word FIRST flashes on in a dark color. When the Women's Basketball Channel is introduced, the screen will flood with action shots of successful plays and triumphant wins.

Speaker: Commanding male voice

Music: Vivaldi's "The Four Seasons"

Mood: Dramatic, creating a sense of importance

Text of Commercial

The first time women are allowed to vote—1869

The first woman senator—Rebecca Feltom, 1922

The first woman to fly solo across the Atlantic Ocean—Amelia Earhart, 1932

The first American woman astronaut—Sally Ride, 1983

The first time the Women's Basketball Association has its own channel—NOW! Be one of the FIRST to see professional women's basketball on WBC.

Persuasive Writing © 1998 Creative Teaching Press

Commercial
Sample 2

THE SPRINKLO-MATIC HEAD GADGET

Student Author: Jordon Henderson

Staging Information

Setting/Overview: (30-second radio commercial) High-energy radio announcer describing the many benefits of the Sprinklo-Matic Head Gadget

Speaker: Upbeat, energetic male voice

Music: Running theme from the film Rocky

Mood: Circus atmosphere, high energy

Text of Commercial

Joggers, sports fans, farmers, and gardeners—here's a new product that will revolutionize the lifestyles of the hot and sweaty forever!

It's a breakthrough in design technology. It's the never-before-seen Sprinklo-Matic Head Gadget!

No more having to wait to get home to have that cool, refreshing shower. You can take it with you. Just fill up the water pouch with cool water before you leave the house. Then when you are out in the garden, or at a sporting event, and all of a sudden you realize, "Man, I'm hot!", just press the button and cool jets of liquid heaven will shower down on your steaming body.

The Sprinklo-Matic Head Gadget comes in many different colors and sizes. It comes in styles for men, women, children, and even household pets. And with only three easy payments of $7.49 each, who can resist the Sprinklo-Matic Head Gadget? Get yours today!

Persuasive Writing © 1998 Creative Teaching Press

Name: _____

Commercial Frame

1. PRODUCT NAME: _____

2. STAGING INFORMATION: _____

3. SETTING/OVERVIEW:

    a. Actors or Spokespeople: _____

    b. Background Music or Sounds: _____

    c. Mood: _____

4. PERSUASIVE LANGUAGE/ADVERTISING TECHNIQUES:

    a. _____

    b. _____

5. PROPAGANDA TECHNIQUES:

    a. _____

    b. _____

TEXT:

Persuasive Writing © 1998 Creative Teaching Press

Writer's Name: _____   Evaluator's Name: _____

Commercial Rubric

	Great!	O.K.	Needs Help
Critical Components			
Provides positive information about a person, product, or service			
Uses persuasive language and advertising techniques (catchy name, special features, sense of urgency, affordable prices)			
Uses propaganda techniques ("loaded" words, endorsement, glittering generalities, bandwagon, name calling, plain folks)			
Provides staging information (setting/overview, actors or spokespeople, music, mood), listed before the text of the commercial itself			
Short and concise			
Style			
Word Choice			
Strong, active verbs			
Precise words			
Words that evoke imagery and sensory detail			
Writing devices such as alliteration, metaphor, simile, onomatopoeia, and personification			
Coherence			
Clearly presented ideas			
Logically sequenced ideas			
Other Considerations			
Originality			
Characterization			
Dialogue			
Mechanics			
Ending punctuation			
Capitalization			
Comma rules			
Quotation marks			
Paragraph structure			

Persuasive Essay

Critical Components

A persuasive essay states an opinion about a particular subject and attempts to persuade the reader to accept that opinion. A persuasive essay uses persuasive language techniques (see page 48). A persuasive essay is composed of three major sections:

- an introduction that includes an interesting opening and a thesis statement that summarizes the main reason for the opinion

- a body that includes a paragraph, supported by facts and examples, for each main idea

- a conclusion constituting a brief restatement of the main idea

Preparation

Locate persuasive essays (in the form of editorials) in your local newspaper. Pick an issue that would be of interest to your students, such as lengthening the academic school year, students or teachers choosing seating arrangements, or making school uniforms mandatory. Make overhead transparencies of pages 48 and 50. Photocopy pages 47 and 49–51 for students.

Setting the Stage

Ask students to express their opinions about a current issue, such as lowering the voting age. Allow time for a brief discussion and then tally student opinions on the board.

Next, read aloud an editorial addressing this issue. Ask students to again express their opinions about this same issue. Tally students' opinions. Did the persuasive editorial change any opinions? If so, how? Have students identify specific words, phrases, and arguments that were influential in changing their opinion. Stress the power and importance of the written word to communicate with and persuade others.

Instructional Input

1. Distribute copies of the Persuasive Essay Building Blocks reproducible (page 47). Discuss the three main sections of a persuasive essay.

2. After you have taught and discussed each major building block, provide pairs of students with a copy of the Persuasive Essay Sample (page 49). Have student pairs identify and label the persuasive writing building blocks (introduction, body, and conclusion) in the essay.

3. Tell students that when writing a persuasive essay, their writing will be more effective if they use specific persuasive writing techniques. Use the overhead transparency of page 48 to teach these specific techniques. After you have discussed the techniques, instruct students to locate and label the techniques that the author used in his essay.

Guided Practice

1. Brainstorm and record on the board topics about which students may wish to write, such as lowering the driving age, extending the academic school year, or laws that mandate recycling.

2. As a class, select one of these topics. Display the overhead transparency of the Persuasive Essay Frame (page 50). Work with this frame together as a class, developing an outline for a persuasive essay. If necessary, invite students to research the topic so they can provide more substantial arguments in the essay.

Independent Practice

1. Depending on the ability level of your class, invite students to write persuasive essays from the outline developed in class or to choose a new topic. Either way, encourage the use of the Persuasive Essay Frame to help students write effectively.

2. Encourage self-, peer, and teacher evaluations using the Persuasive Essay Rubric (page 51).

• Regulated Mountain Lion-Hunting •
Student Author: Brian Johnson

attention grabber

Picture this—you're out in the woods, jogging casually down a hiking trail, experiencing a sense of freedom. Just you, the woods, the fresh air, and an unknown predator stalking you, watching every move you make. You stop to tie your shoe for just a second, making the mistake that triggers the predator-prey instinct of your stalker. By bending over, you briefly resemble an animal on all four legs, and your stalker, a mountain lion, immediately pounces, beginning

loaded word

his (fatal) attack. This is a true, real-life incident that occurred in 1994 in Northern California. The underlying reason for the attack—the area was over-populated with mountain lions. Because an overabundance of these predatory creatures is dangerous to the human population as well as to the deer population, I believe there should be a regulated hunt for mountain lions.

introduction

thesis sentence

Presentation

- Invite students to practice their persuasive essays aloud before presenting them to the class or a small group. If possible, partner students with classmates who hold the opposite opinion and have them take turns sharing their arguments. Then, give the class an opportunity to vote for the opinions they agree with and express what factors influenced their opinion.

- Create a "Current Issues" binder that covers current topics of interest to your students (for example, school-rule issues, ecology issues, and education issues). Encourage students to scan newspapers and magazines for articles about these issues. As students write persuasive essays, have them insert a copy into the binder. Make this binder available to all students for ready reference, for sustained silent reading, for research references, and for parents during Back-to-School Night or Open House.

Teaching Tips/Extensions

- Encourage students to bring to class additional examples of persuasive writing. Stress the importance of using the dictionary and other reference books when reading editorials so that the meanings of words are clearly understood. For example, if students read that Governor X is a liberal, they must understand what a liberal is. Similarly, point out the importance of being a wise consumer of reading materials, checking content against what they know to be true, comparing content with other sources, and avoiding being unduly influenced by other's opinions.

- Have students practice distinguishing fact from opinion. Provide small groups of students with a variety of newspaper clippings, such as advertisements, front-page news articles, and editorials. Ask students to fold a piece of paper in half and label one side *Fact* and the other *Opinion*. Then, have them record sentences and phrases from the articles in the appropriate columns.

Persuasive Essay Building Blocks

INTRODUCTION

1. Start with an attention-grabber such as a question, quote, or humorous or emotional story that captures your reader's attention and compels him or her to continue reading.

2. State your thesis sentence. This is the sentence that summarizes the main reasons for your opinion. This sentence can be placed anywhere in the introduction. It is often the last sentence of this paragraph.

BODY

1. Write one paragraph for each of your main ideas. If you have three main ideas, include three paragraphs in the body of your essay.

2. Each paragraph should have a topic sentence that supports the thesis and states the main idea of that paragraph.

3. The remaining sentences in the paragraph should include facts and examples that support your opinion. Your opinion is a personal judgment or belief that cannot be proven right or wrong. However, you can support your opinion with facts. Your purpose is to provide readers with information that will convince them that your opinions make sense.

CONCLUSION

The conclusion is the final paragraph of a persuasive essay. Restate the thesis and emphasize the most important points. Urge readers to share your opinion and take action to support it.

Persuasive Essay Techniques

ORDER OF INFORMATION

Decide which of your arguments is most important. Then, begin with a clearly defined statement of opinion, support that statement with convincing facts, and end with your strongest ideas. Saving the best for last will create a more lasting impact on your reader.

ANALYZE FACTS AND EXAMPLES

When writing a persuasive essay, include only the facts that support your opinion. Omit facts that do not strengthen your argument.

LOADED WORDS

Always state your opinions and facts honestly, but look for ways to add impact to your words. Loaded words carry an emotional impact and create a sense of urgency. For example, *Pollution is poisoning our planet.*

ANSWER OBJECTIONS

Think of objections that someone might raise against your ideas and provide facts that refute these objections or tell how they can be overcome.

Persuasive Writing © 1998 Creative Teaching Press

Persuasive Essay Sample

• Regulated Mountain-Lion Hunting •

Student Author: Brian Johnson

Picture this—you're out in the woods, jogging casually down a hiking trail, experiencing a sense of freedom. Just you, the woods, the fresh air, and an unknown predator stalking you, watching every move you make. You stop to tie your shoe for just a second, making the mistake that triggers the predator-prey instinct of your stalker. By bending over, you briefly resemble an animal on all four legs, and your stalker, a mountain lion, immediately pounces, beginning his fatal attack. This is a true, real-life incident that occurred in 1994 in Northern California. The underlying reason for the attack—the area was over-populated with mountain lions. Because an overabundance of these predatory creatures is dangerous to the human population as well as to the deer population, I believe there should be a regulated hunt for mountain lions.

A regulated hunt would control the large numbers of mountain lions and protect innocent joggers, campers, and naturalists. The mountain lion has no natural predator; if laws forbid people to hunt mountain lions, how can the population be controlled? The available natural food supply for the lions will be insufficient and attacks on humans will continue.

Regulated mountain-lion hunts would also protect our dwindling deer population. A single mountain lion can eat two deer in a week (eight in a month). Just think how many deer are consumed in a year by a population of 1,000 mountain lions.

Mountain-lion hunting should not be a free-for-all. We should regulate it just like we do deer hunting. We want to control the population, not hunt them to extinction. In this way, the mountain lion and deer populations would be stabilized.

I believe we should do what's best for us, the deer, and the mountain lions. We should have regulated mountain-lion hunts that would control their numbers while protecting innocent human beings as well as the deer population.

Name: _____

Persuasive Essay Frame

Thesis Statement:

Attention-Grabbers:

Order of Importance

_____

Main Idea #1

Topic Sentence: _____

_____

Supporting Details: _____

_____

Loaded Language: _____

_____

_____

Main Idea #2

Topic Sentence: _____

_____

Supporting Details: _____

_____

Loaded Language: _____

_____

_____

Main Idea #3

Topic Sentence: _____

_____

Supporting Details: _____

_____

Loaded Language: _____

_____

Conclusion: _____

_____

Persuasive Writing © 1998 Creative Teaching Press

Persuasive Essay Rubric

	Great!	O.K.	Needs Help
Critical Components			
States an opinion and attempts to persuade			
Includes an introduction, a body, and a conclusion			
Includes an attention-grabber in the introduction			
Thesis statement summarizes the main reason for the opinion			
Includes a paragraph supported by facts and examples for each main idea			
Includes a brief restatement of the main idea as a conclusion			
Uses persuasive language techniques such as loaded language, ordered information, answered objections, and analyzed facts			
Style			
Word Choice Strong, active verbs			
Precise words			
Words that evoke imagery and sensory detail			
Writing devices such as alliteration, metaphor, simile, onomatopoeia, and personification			
Coherence Clearly presented ideas			
Logically sequenced ideas			
Originality			
Mechanics			
Ending punctuation			
Capitalization			
Comma rules			
Quotation marks			
Paragraph structure			

Campaign Speech

Critical Components

A campaign speech includes a self-introduction of the speaker, including his or her name and the office for which he or she is running. A campaign speech includes a vivid description of why the speaker is qualified for the job. A campaign speech includes a description of current problems and how the speaker will solve these problems. A campaign speech includes a closing.

Preparation

Gather videotaped clips of campaign speeches or be prepared to model a brief campaign speech. Ask local school board or city council members for copies of their successful campaign speeches to share with students. Make an overhead transparency of page 55. Photocopy pages 56 and 57 for students.

Setting the Stage

Ask students to discuss what they know about the purpose of campaign speeches. Define a campaign speech as a persuasive speech given by an individual running for a political office. Ask if any students have heard a campaign speech at school or on television. Play video clips, read a real campaign speech, or ask an older student who has run for a student-body office to recite his or her speech in front of your class.

Instructional Input

1. After students watch and listen to a few campaign speeches, explain that the intent of a campaign speech is to influence voters' decisions. There are at least four key components of a campaign speech:

   a. an introduction that includes the candidate's name and the office for which he or she is running

   b. a description of the candidate's qualifications that explains why he or she can do a good job

   c. a description of current problems and how the candidate plans to solve them

   d. a polite, friendly closing in which the candidate repeats his or her name and the office for which he or she is running

2. Rerun the video clips and/or ask the student officer to model his or her speech again. Have students identify the key components of a campaign speech as they listen and watch.

Guided Practice

1. Brainstorm school offices for which students could run.

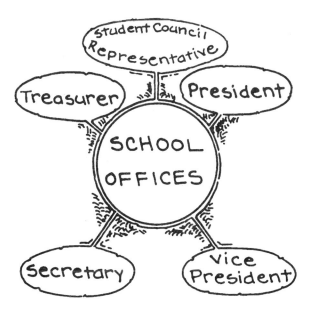

2. You may also want to brainstorm political offices, such as School Board Member, Mayor, Governor, or President.

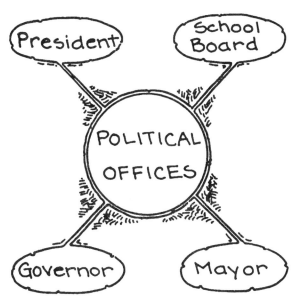

3. Show the overhead transparency of page 55. Help students identify the critical components in this student-authored campaign speech.

● **Campaign Speech** ●

Student Author: Shaheema Shaw

introduction [Hello, my name is Shaheema Shaw. I am running for the Board of Education.] States office

I have many qualifications for this position. I am from an educated family. I am widely traveled. I am familiar with many cultures. I have been both a teacher and a principal. } qualifications

Problems she can solve
We have a lot of problems in our school. One of the problems is that many good teachers leave this school. I will solve this so they will stay here for a long time. I will make sure the teachers get the salaries they deserve. Also, I will find quality teachers who will teach our children the value of discipline and hard work.

Another problem is that we have too much crime in our schools. I will solve this by helping everyone carefully protect their belongings. We will discipline anyone who steals from our schools. We will all work together.

Once again, my name is Shaheema Shaw. Please vote for me for the Board of Education.] closing

Independent Practice

1. Give students copies of the Campaign Speech Frame (page 56). Ask them to brainstorm and list on this form the critical components of the speech they will write.

2. Encourage students to use the frame as a prewriting guide to write a rough draft.

3. Distribute copies of the Campaign Speech Rubric (page 57). Encourage self-critiquing with this rubric.

4. After self-critiquing, revising, and editing, encourage students to gather at least three other readers to critique their writing against the rubric. Have students make changes based upon suggestions and then present their final draft to you.

Presentation

- Invite students to present their campaign speeches to the class. Discuss the importance of personal appearances and invite students to dress formally on the day of their speeches.

- Have students place copies of their speeches in a class binder under headings that correspond to the offices for which they ran, such as Student Body Representative and Class President. Provide this binder as a reference tool for students who give speeches in the future.

Teaching Hints/Extensions

- If possible, show students a videotape of the 1960 presidential debate between Richard Nixon and John Kennedy. Then, discuss how the candidates' personal appearance might have affected the outcome of the election.

- If several students write campaign speeches for the same office, have the class take a mock vote for the person who was most influential in convincing them that they could do the job the best.

- Save copies of your best speeches for next year's lessons. Ask students to come back to your class next year and give their campaign speeches for the Setting the Stage portion of your lesson.

Campaign Speech Sample

Student Author: Shaheema Shaw

Hello, my name is Shaheema Shaw. I am running for the Board of Education.

I have many qualifications for this position. I am from an educated family. I am widely traveled. I am familiar with many cultures. I have been both a teacher and a principal.

We have a lot of problems in our school. One of the problems is that many good teachers leave this school. I will solve this so they will stay here for a long time. I will make sure the teachers get the salaries they deserve. Also, I will find quality teachers who will teach our children the value of discipline and hard work.

Another problem is that we have too much crime in our schools. I will solve this by helping everyone carefully protect their belongings. We will discipline anyone who steals from our schools. We will all work together.

Once again, my name is Shaheema Shaw. Please vote for me for the Board of Education.

Name: _____

Campaign Speech Frame

1. Introduction—your name and the office for which you are running

_____

2. Qualifications

   a. _____

   b. _____

   c. _____

3. Problems and Solutions—specific problems the voting community is experiencing and ways you are going to solve or change those problems

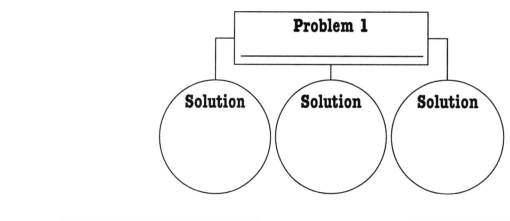

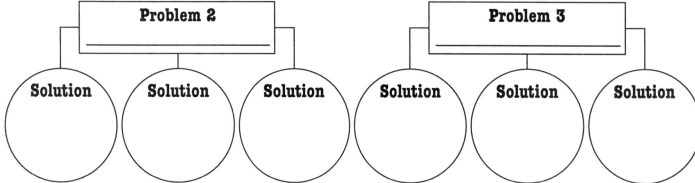

4. Closing—restate your name and the office for which you are running

_____

Persuasive Writing © 1998 Creative Teaching Press

Writer's Name: _____   Evaluator's Name: _____

Campaign Speech Rubric

	Great!	O.K.	Needs Help
Critical Components			
Introduction			
Includes name of speaker			
Includes name of office for which the speaker is running			
Body			
Includes qualifications			
Includes description of current problems and how they will be solved or changed			
Closing			
Includes restatement of speaker's name			
Includes restatement of office for which speaker is running			
Style			
Word Choice			
Strong, active verbs			
Precise words			
Words that evoke imagery and sensory detail			
Coherence			
Clearly presented ideas			
Logically sequenced ideas			
Originality			
Mechanics			
Ending punctuation			
Capitalization			
Comma rules			
Quotation marks			
Paragraph structure			

Persuasive Letter

Critical Components

A persuasive letter includes the date and a greeting. A persuasive letter opens with a positive statement. A persuasive letter includes a "however" statement that leads into a concern. A persuasive letter suggests an action plan and the benefits of this plan. A persuasive letter ends with a positive and encouraging statement.

Preparation

Make an overhead transparency of page 61. Photocopy pages 62 and 63 for students.

Setting the Stage

Ask students to discuss times they have been upset or bothered by a situation that they wish could have been handled differently. Categorize and record these ideas on the board. Then, have students suggest ways these problems could have been changed or solved. Finally, ask students to name some methods for communicating their feelings about problems and solutions, such as those they discussed. When students suggest verbal communication as a method, explain that talking may not be convincing or memorable enough to persuade someone to address their concerns. Discuss the benefits of writing persuasive letters in these situations.

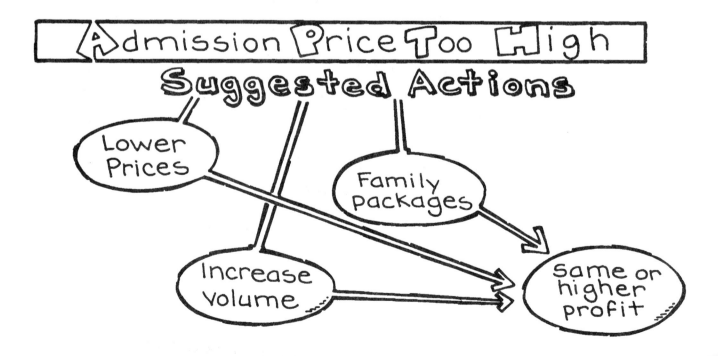

Instructional Input

1. Display the critical components of a persuasive letter on a chart, overhead projector, or blackboard.

2. Show students the overhead transparency of page 61. Ask students to mark each component with an overhead pen.

3. Discuss why each component is important. Be sure to mention that a positive opening statement puts the reader at ease. The "however" is the bridge that leads into the real issue. The action plan provides a positive way to change the problem and prevents the letter from simply expressing a complaint. Ending on a positive note tells the reader that you have confidence that he or she can solve the problem.

October 31, 1997 ←date

Dear Crispy Bite Potato Chip Company, ← greeting

positive statement

(Thank you for continuing to produce delicious potato chips.)

Whenever I am hungry for a snack, I always choose Crispy Bite potato chips. The barbecue flavor is my favorite. (However,) I feel that your
HOWEVER
small snack-size bags do not contain enough chips. I am always very excited to open a new bag and then disappointed when I find that it is barely half full. I don't feel like I am getting my money's worth. Could you fill the bags a little more or make the size of the package smaller? Maybe a smaller package would enable you to lower the price.

action plan

positive closing

Your company has always produced a high-quality product that I and all my friends enjoy. I thought you would want to know about our problem with the amount of chips in your bags because I am sure you are interested in your customers' opinions.

Thanks for your attention and your delicious chips.

Sincerely,

Allison

Guided Practice

1. As a class, compose a letter of concern. Use one of the student-suggested topics as the issue of concern.

2. After completing the letter, have students identify the key components. If any components have been omitted, revise the letter until it meets the criteria.

Independent Practice

1. Ask students to choose their own topics and to compose their own letter of concern. Give students a copy of the Persuasive Letter Frame (page 62) to help them organize their ideas and begin prewriting.

2. Encourage students to self-critique their first drafts using the Persuasive Letter Rubric (page 63).

3. Divide students into cooperative groups and have them critique each other's letters using the criteria described in the rubric.

Presentation

• If students have written letters to actual people or organizations, invite them to mail the letters to the appropriate address. Be sure to model the format for addressing an envelope.

• Display final drafts, when appropriate, on a bulletin board titled *Caring Enough to Communicate Concerns.*

Teaching Hints/Extensions

• Repeat this lesson using various themes, such as suggestions regarding changes in behavior, changes to business products or services, and changes in the law.

• This lesson may evoke topics of a personal nature regarding students' relationships. Take care to maintain confidentiality and do not post these letters without students' permission.

Persuasive Letter Sample

October 31, 1997

Dear Crispy Bite Potato Chip Company,

Thank you for continuing to produce delicious potato chips. Whenever I am hungry for a snack, I always choose Crispy Bite potato chips. The barbecue flavor is my favorite. However, I feel that your small snack-size bags do not contain enough chips. I am always very excited to open a new bag and then disappointed when I find that it is barely half full. I don't feel like I am getting my money's worth. Could you fill the bags a little more or make the size of the package smaller? Maybe a smaller package would enable you to lower the price.

Your company has always produced a high-quality product that I and all my friends enjoy. I thought you would want to know about our problem with the amount of chips in your bags because I am sure you are interested in your customers' opinions.

Thanks for your attention and your delicious chips.

Sincerely,

Allison

Name: _____

Persuasive Letter Frame

What do you want to change?

To whom could you write to help you make this change?

What positive statement could you include before offering your suggestion?

HOWEVER,

State your concern.

Describe a plan of action.

End with a positive statement.

Include a friendly closing.

Persuasive Letter Rubric

	Great!	O.K.	Needs Help
Critical Components			
Introduction Includes the date			
Includes a greeting			
Begins with a positive statement			
Body Includes a "however" statement that leads into a concern			
Includes a suggested plan of action that addresses the concern			
Closing Ends on a positive note			
Includes a formal closing and signature			
Style			
Word Choice Strong, active verbs			
Precise words			
Coherence Clearly presented ideas			
Logically sequenced ideas			
Other Considerations			
Originality			
Persuasive phrases			
Mechanics			
Ending punctuation			
Capitalization			
Comma rules			
Quotation marks			
Paragraph structure			

Bibliography

Batzle, Janine. *Portfolio Assessment and Evaluation.* Creative Teaching Press, 1992. How to develop and use portfolios in K–6 classrooms.

Elbow, Peter. *Writing with Power: Techniques for Mastering the Writing Process.* Oxford University Press, 1981. A self-help resource book for adults who want to improve their writing.

Flynn, Kris. *Graphic Organizers.* Creative Teaching Press, 1995. Visual aides to help children organize their thinking and writing.

Graves, Donald H. *A Fresh Look at Writing.* Heinemann, 1994. A professional writing book for teachers, with fundamentals for broadening children's writing repertoires.

McCarthy, Tara. *150 Thematic Writing Activities.* Scholastic, 1993. Reproducible reading and writing motivators for students with diverse interests and learning strengths.

Miller, Wilma H. *Alternative Assessment Techniques for Reading & Writing.* Center for Applied Research in Education, 1995. Simple and practical assessment techniques with reproducible tools.

Schifferle, Judith. *Editorial Skills.* Center for Applied Research in Education, Inc., 1985. Reproducible activities for helping students sharpen their editorial skills.

Schifferle, Judith. *Word Skills.* Center for Applied Research in Education, Inc., 1985. Reproducible activities to help students expand their writing vocabulary.

Sparks, J.E. *Write for Power.* Communication Associates, 1995. Step-by-step procedures to help strengthen children's writing.

Sunflower, Cherlyn. *Really Writing! Ready-to-Use Writing Process Activities for the Elementary Grades.* Center for Applied Research in Education, 1994. Creative writing lessons in the narrative, expressive, informative, and persuasive domains.